THE

NEW TESTAMENT CHALLENGE

STUDY JOURNAL

THE

NEW TESTAMENT CHALLENGE

AN EIGHT-WEEK JOURNEY THROUGH THE STORY OF JESUS, HIS CHURCH, AND HIS RETURN

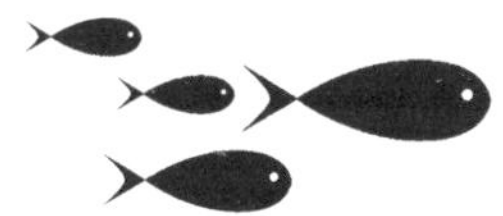

STUDY JOURNAL | EIGHT SESSIONS

The New Testament Challenge Study Journal

This title is also available as a Zondervan ebook. Requests for information should be addressed to:

Zondervan, 3900 Sparks Dr. SE, Grand Rapids, Michigan 49546

ISBN 978-0-310-12503-7 (softcover)

ISBN 978-0-310-12504-4 (ebook)

First Printing November 2020 / Printed in the United States of America

Contents

How to Use This Guide

What would happen if you actually *read* the New Testament? Not just a verse here or there, but every part of the New Testament, in its entirety? And what if, instead of going it alone, you had real conversations about the Bible—ones that anyone could join regardless of where they were in their faith journey? *The New Testament Challenge* is about reading the Bible as it was meant to be read—whole books, in community. It will take you beyond Bible study, beyond reading in fragments, and beyond reading in isolation. It will help you discover the complete story.

AN INVITATION

During this study you and your fellow group members will be exploring the New Testament in its *entirety*. The New Testament is the second of the two major divisions in the Bible, filling the final one-quarter of its pages. It continues the story, begun in the Old Testament, of how God is restoring his original purpose in creation by working through the chosen people of Israel.

The New Testament tells how this story reached its crowning moment during the first century AD as Jesus of Nazareth, Israel's Messiah, answered the question of who God is and what he is like once and for all. Through his teaching, Jesus revealed the deepest meaning of the laws and institutions that God had given to the people of Israel. Through his death and resurrection, Jesus introduced the forgiveness and life of the age to come into the present age.

The New Testament also tells how the followers of Jesus formed a new community and invited people from all over the world to join them. It describes how they worked together to live out the reign of God that Jesus had announced and begun. Finally, the New Testament looks ahead to the day when Jesus will return to renew all of creation and to establish God's justice and peace throughout the earth.

HOW IT WORKS

The New Testament Challenge will require you to take three key steps: (1) read big, (2) read real, and (3) read together.

1. **Read big.** During the course of this study, you will cover the entire New Testament in eight weeks, reading five days a week, or around twelve pages a day. Each day's average reading will take thirty minutes or so for you to complete.
2. **Read real.** You will use a groundbreaking presentation of the Scriptures called *The Books of the Bible,* which has been designed to feel more like reading the original.
3. **Read together.** You will meet with your discussion group once a week for book club-style conversations about the Bible.

A UNIQUE BIBLE

As noted, during this study you will read from a revolutionary presentation of the New Testament called *The Books of the Bible.* When you open your copy, the first thing you will notice is that this is no ordinary Bible. There are no chapter or verse numbers. No study notes or cross references. No red lettering.

This is because none of these features are original to the Scriptures. Most were added centuries later to help us find things. But the Bible isn't a reference book. First and foremost, it's a story. It's a collection of books, each of which was meant to be experienced as a whole. Modern Bible formatting imposes a different structure on the text, one that encourages us to read in fragments. But *The Books of the Bible* is designed to be read from beginning to end. So we've stripped away centuries of artificial formatting, leaving behind nothing but pure Bible text in a presentation that's easier to read and understand.

We've formatted each book in the New Testament so you can see the natural section breaks put there by the authors. We've also rearranged the books for easier understanding—for example, putting Paul's letters in a more chronological order (instead of longest to shortest), so you can follow along more easily. *The Books of the Bible* features the complete text of the New Testament using the New International Version®, the most widely read contemporary English translation of the Bible.

FIVE TIPS FOR READING

1. **Read what you can.** Don't get discouraged if you fall behind. Keep at it, even if you don't make it all the way through each day's reading. If you have trouble keeping up, listening to the audio version can help.
2. **Read every day.** Plan on reading five days a week, Monday through Friday. Note that some daily readings will be longer or shorter because each one ends at the close of a book or a natural section break within a book. The pace is a little intense, but reading large portions of Scripture is also incredibly rewarding. So be fully present.
3. **Avoid distraction while reading.** (Turns out we're not that good at multitasking.) Instead, devote your full attention to the text.

4. **Read the book introductions.** *The Books of the Bible* includes brief introductions or "invitations" to each book of the New Testament, unpacking the context and literary structure of what you're about to read. Trust us, they are well worth your time.
5. **Don't worry about the parts you don't understand.** The goal is to read big, not to catch every detail. You can always go back and study a specific passage in greater detail later. For now, take in the big picture. Let that be your focus as you read.

PLANNING YOUR WEEKLY GATHERINGS

Your small group should meet once a week during *The New Testament Challenge*. If possible, plan to meet on the weekends. There are no readings assigned for Saturday and Sunday, which makes the weekend a good time to get together.

The New Testament Challenge is broken into eight weeks of readings, but **plan on meeting nine times.** You will want to have an introductory gathering the week before you start reading, and then meet once a week for the next eight weeks to discuss the readings.

Most discussion groups meet for sixty to ninety minutes each week, but feel free to adjust this schedule based on the needs of your group. Spend the first 30 to 60 minutes of your group time sharing your reflections on the text you read during the week. Use these five simple conversation starters to get the discussions flowing:

1. What was new or compelling to you?
2. What questions did you have?
3. Was there anything that bothered you?
4. What did you learn about loving God?
5. What did you learn about loving others?

During the last fifteen to thirty minutes of your meeting, you will prepare for the week ahead by watching a video from Jeff Manion. **Be sure not to skip this step,** as the material Jeff presents will give you and your group members important background information to the passages you will be reading during the week. Note that a brief outline of the topics and concepts that Jeff presents has been included in this guide to help you follow along, and space has also been provided for you to write down your thoughts. Discuss any questions or personal insights that come out of this time of teaching with your group.

THREE TIPS FOR WEEKLY GATHERINGS

If you have been part of a Bible study before, you might find these gatherings a bit different. Here are three tips to help you get the most from them.

TIP #1: THINK "BOOK CLUB"

Treat your weekly gatherings more like a book club than a traditional Bible study. The discussions are meant to be free-flowing and wide-ranging.

You may come to each week's gathering with lots of questions. That's okay. It's what happens when you read twelve pages a day! Try to focus your conversation on the big picture—where the overall story is moving and the part you are invited to play in it. To help, you can suggest your group keeps a "parking lot" list of questions to explore further after your journey.

TIP #2: HONOR EVERY PARTICIPANT

It's likely your fellow group members come from a variety of backgrounds. You may hold different perspectives or assumptions about the Bible. Some of you may be lifelong students of the text. Others may be brand new to it. Regardless, it is important to remember that each person has something meaningful to add to the conversation.

TIP #3: LISTEN ACTIVELY AND SPEAK FREELY

Welcome every voice in the conversation, and don't hesitate to add your own. You never know how someone else might benefit by hearing what was new or compelling to you, what questions you had, or what you wrestled with during your reading of the New Testament.

ADDITIONAL RESOURCES

Thank you for your participation in this group and for accepting *The New Testament Challenge.* If you are a group leader, note there are additional resources for you at the end of this study journal on how to structure your time together and get the most out of your discussion times.

INTRODUCTORY SESSION

This opening introductory session introduces your group to *The New Testament Challenge*. Hold this session the week before your first meeting.

GETTING TO KNOW YOU (15–30 minutes)

If your group members are new to each other, invite each person to introduce himself or herself, using any or all of the following prompts:

- What are three roles in your life, and what do you like about them?
- What one word describes your past experience of reading the Bible?
- What do you hope to get from this journey?

INTRODUCTION (15–30 minutes)

Begin by discussing the information covered in pages vii–xii of this study journal. In particular, you will want to review the following key sections together:

- Five Tips for Reading
- Planning Your Weekly Gatherings
- Three Tips for Weekly Gatherings

Allow time for discussion about how your group wants to function with each other and to address any concerns people have about doing the Bible reading. Next, if time allows, read through all of the introductory materials in pages iii–xvii of *The Books of the Bible: New Testament*. If you have time constraints, read just "The Drama of the Bible in Six Acts," beginning on page i, and "Invitation to the New Testament," beginning on page xv.

PREPARING FOR THE WEEK AHEAD (15–20 minutes)

Next, discuss the challenge of reading twelve pages a day. Remember that most readings will take around thirty minutes to complete—about the same time it takes to watch a TV show. Finally, to get the most out of what you will be reading during the coming week, close your time by watching the video of week 1, in which Jeff Manion **introduces the New Testament** and explains the themes and relevance of **Luke**. Use the following outline to write down any insights or questions.

WHAT IS THE NEW TESTAMENT?

The Old Testament asks, how can the presence of God be restored?

In the New Testament, there is something new: God himself enters the planet in Jesus.

The New Testament has twenty-seven books:

- The Gospels (four books)
- The Book of Acts
- The Epistles (twenty-one books)
- The Book of Revelation

As you read, keep the first-century audience in mind: "What did it mean to them?" Then ask, "What does it mean to me?"

The New Testament was written by nine human authors and the Divine Author.

LUKE

Gospel: means "good news"

Themes of Luke

Early events of Jesus's life

Women: first-century world was very patriarchal

Meals

Holy Spirit

Relevance of Luke

How might God be calling your voice?

THIS WEEK

Read the book of Luke–Acts in *The Books of the Bible: New Testament*. Maintain your momentum by keeping these guidelines in mind:

- Read what you can.
- Read something every day.
- Always have your *Books of the Bible* with you.
- Remember every week is a new week.
- Use this study journal as you do your reading for week 1: Luke–Acts, recording any thoughts on the Daily Reading Journal pages.

WEEK 1
LUKE–ACTS

LUKE

The two volumes of Luke–Acts have been combined in *The Books of the Bible* and placed first because they provide an overview of the entire New Testament period. Luke wrote this two-volume history to serve several important purposes:

- He wanted to assure followers of Jesus that what they had been taught about him was trustworthy.
- He wanted to document how God kept the promise he made to the people of Israel by sending them their long-awaited Messiah, demonstrating that the true God is faithful and can be trusted completely.
- He wanted to prove that the extension of God's blessings to the Gentiles is not a fickle change of plans but rather the masterful fulfillment of a plan God has been pursuing over the ages.

What to watch for in Luke: Look for some unlikely cast members in Luke's drama. Luke highlights Jesus's compassion toward the outsiders and outcasts of his day: the poor, the disabled, tax collectors, women, children, and others. According to Luke, Jesus is for everybody.

PERSONAL BIBLE EXPERIENCE

Your personal Bible experience starts with a daily practice of reading the Bible. This week before your group meeting, read the book of Luke. Use the journaling space to capture your thoughts, questions, responses, emotions, and insights as you read the daily selection. Keep in mind the following questions you will be talking about with your discussion group:

- What was new or compelling to you?
- What questions did you have?
- Was there anything that bothered you?
- What did you learn about loving God?
- What did you learn about loving others?

DAILY READING JOURNAL

Day 1: Luke–Acts Invitation–Luke 4:13 (pages 1–11)

Day 2: Luke 4:14–9:50 (pages 12–25)

Day 3: Luke 9:51–13:21 (pages 25–34)

Day 4: Luke 13:22–19:27 (pages 34–44)

Day 5: Luke 19:28–24:53 (pages 44–56)

COMMUNITY BIBLE EXPERIENCE

You have been experiencing the Bible personally by reading through the book of Luke this week. Now, take some time as a group to reflect on what you have learned.

REFLECTING ON THE PREVIOUS WEEK (30–60 minutes)

Based on your Personal Bible Experience in Luke this week, have a conversation with your group about what you read by answering the following questions:

What was new or compelling to you?

What questions did you have?

Was there anything that bothered you?

What did you learn about loving God?

What did you learn about loving others?

PREPARING FOR THE WEEK AHEAD (15–20 minutes)

To get the most out of what you will be reading in the coming week, close your time together by watching the video for week 2, in which Jeff Manion explains the themes and relevance of **Acts** and **1–2 Thessalonians**. Use the following outline to write down any insights or questions.

ACTS

What the disciples did after Jesus ascended

Key to Acts: Movement

> But you will receive power when the Holy Spirit comes on you; and you will be my witnesses in Jerusalem, and in all Judea and Samaria, and to the ends of the earth.
> (Acts 1:8)

Key Event: At Pentecost, the Spirit descends

Key Picture of Transformation: Community

Key Lesson: God is at work in our disappointment

Key Figure: Saul

> [Saul] fell to the ground and heard a voice say to him, "Saul, Saul, why do you persecute me?" "Who are you, Lord?" Saul asked. "I am Jesus, whom you are persecuting," he replied. (Acts 9:4–5)

Key City: Antioch

Themes of Acts

Places

Sermons

Conflict and persecution

Movement of the Holy Spirit

Relevance of Acts

Jesus wants to be known

1–2 THESSALONIANS

Purpose of 1–2 Thessalonians

To encourage the Thessalonians in their faith

Themes of 1–2 Thessalonians

Encouragement in their suffering

Make a clean break from their old life, and step into their new life

Comfort

THIS WEEK

Read Acts from the book of Luke–Acts and 1–2 Thessalonians in *The Books of the Bible: New Testament*. Maintain your momentum by keeping these guidelines in mind:

- Read what you can.
- Read something every day.
- Always have your *Books of the Bible* with you.
- Remember every week is a new week.
- Use this study journal as you do your reading for week 2: Luke–Acts, 1–2 Thessalonians, recording any thoughts on the Daily Reading Journal pages.

WEEK 2
LUKE–ACTS, 1 & 2 THESSALONIANS

ACTS

While Luke's first volume tracked Jesus as he worked his way toward Jerusalem where he gave his life and then rose again, Luke's second volume, Acts, follows the community of Jesus-followers outward from Jerusalem as they expand and spread the good news to Asia, Europe, and eventually Rome. Acts has six parts, each which describes a successive phase in the expansion of the community of Jesus's followers outward from Jerusalem:

- In the first phase, the community is established in Jerusalem and becomes Greek-speaking, enabling it to spread its message throughout the empire.
- In the second phase, the community expands into the rest of Palestine.
- In the third phase, Gentiles are included in the community along with Jews.
- In the fourth phase, the community intentionally sends messengers westward into the populous Roman province of Asia.
- In the fifth phase, these messengers enter Europe.
- In the final phase, the community reaches all the way to the capital of Rome and into the highest levels of society.

What to watch for in Acts: Notice how God uses hardship to advance the good news about Jesus. In Acts, the church's expansion beyond Jerusalem is a direct result of religious persecution that backfires.

1–2 THESSALONIANS

These are among Paul's earliest letters. In his first letter to the new church at Thessalonica (in modern-day Greece), Paul encourages believers to hold on to their faith despite intense opposition. He recalls his time with them and says how grateful he is that they've remained faithful to Jesus. He then transitions to provide instruction on several practical matters:

- Paul teaches them to avoid sexual immorality, to love one another, and to work hard and earn their own livings.
- Paul explains that believers who die before the coming of the Lord are not lost. They will be raised from the dead at this public appearance of the Messiah. However, Jesus will come back unexpectedly, so they should live in such a way that they won't be ashamed to greet him.
- Paul advises them on how to live as a community of Jesus followers.

Paul writes his second letter to correct a false report that the "day of the Lord" had come without the vindication the Thessalonians were hoping for. In this short letter:

- Paul reassures them that God will pay back trouble those who have troubled them and give relief to those who are troubled.

- Paul corrects the false report by reminding them of his teachings when he was with them about when the day of the Lord would arrive.
- Paul urges them once again to not live in idleness but to work hard and earn their own livings.

What to watch for in 1–2 Thessalonians: To better appreciate the context of these letters, think back to Paul's experience in Thessalonica with the jealous Jews who rioted, then followed him to Berea and disrupted his efforts again (see pages 86–87). Paul knew the believers in Thessalonica would be facing violent opposition.

PERSONAL BIBLE EXPERIENCE

Your personal Bible experience starts with a daily practice of reading the Bible. This week before your group meeting, read Acts from the book of Luke–Acts, and 1–2 Thessalonians. Use the journaling space to capture your thoughts, questions, responses, emotions, and insights as you read the daily selection. Keep in mind the following questions you will be talking about with your discussion group:

- What was new or compelling to you?
- What questions did you have?
- Was there anything that bothered you?
- What did you learn about loving God?
- What did you learn about loving others?

DAILY READING JOURNAL

Day 6: Acts 1:1–6:7 (pages 57–66)

Day 7: Acts 6:8–12:24 (pages 66–78)

Day 8: Acts 12:25–19:20 (pages 78–90)

Day 9: Acts 19:21–28:31 (pages 90–106)

Day 10: 1 Thessalonians Invitation–2 Thessalonians 3:18 (pages 107–119)

COMMUNITY BIBLE EXPERIENCE

Welcome to week 2 of the Community Bible Experience. You have been experiencing the Bible personally by reading through Acts in the book of Luke–Acts and 1–2 Thessalonians this week, and now your group has gathered to experience the Bible in community with each other. Think of your discussion as more of a book club than a Bible study.

REFLECTING ON THE PREVIOUS WEEK (30–60 minutes)

From your Personal Bible Experience in Luke–Acts and 1–2 Thessalonians this week, have a conversation with your group about what you read by answering the following questions:

What was new or compelling to you?

What questions did you have?

Was there anything that bothered you?

What did you learn about loving God?

What did you learn about loving others?

PREPARING FOR THE WEEK AHEAD (15–20 minutes)

To get the most out of what you will be reading in the coming week, close your time together by watching the video for week 3, in which Jeff Manion explains the themes and relevance of **1–2 Corinthians**, **Galatians**, and **Romans**. Use the following outline to write down any insights or questions.

1 CORINTHIANS

Topics in 1 Corinthians

Gave Paul's answers to the Corinthians' questions:

Can a Christian eat food sacrificed to idols? (In reply, Paul asked, "How does your decision affect other believers? How does it help you love?")

Why is there a resurrection of the body?

Gave Paul's response to Corinthians' problems:

Division, factions, believers suing each other

People were not sharing food during the Lord's Supper.

2 CORINTHIANS

Topics in 2 Corinthians

Paul's defense of his reputation

God's comfort in trials

> Praise be to the God and Father of our Lord Jesus Christ, the Father of compassion and the God of all comfort, who comforts us in all our troubles, so that we can comfort those in any trouble with the comfort we ourselves receive from God.
>
> (2 Corinthians 1:3–4)

Offerings and generosity

> For you know the grace of our Lord Jesus Christ, that though he was rich, yet for your sake he became poor, so that you through his poverty might become rich.
>
> (2 Corinthians 8:9)

GALATIANS

Problem in Galatians

People were from Gentile backgrounds, and Judaizers were confusing them, saying faith in Jesus was insufficient to save.

Key topic in Galatians

Inner transformation and the fruit of the Spirit

ROMANS

Topics in Romans

Central point: Gospel (good news)

Bad news: We are born rebellious

Righteousness: What does it mean for a deeply flawed person to be right with God?

Words describing our new relationship with Christ:

Justification: God declaring guilty people just

Redemption: Set free because of Christ

Sanctification: Learning to live the new life

Relevance of Romans

Fresh encounter with God's love, mercy, and grace

THIS WEEK

Read the books of 1–2 Corinthians, Galatians, and half of Romans in *The Books of the Bible: New Testament*. Maintain your momentum by keeping these guidelines in mind:

- Read what you can.
- Read something every day.
- Always have your *Books of the Bible* with you.
- Remember every week is a new week.
- Use this study journal as you do your reading for week 3: 1–2 Corinthians, Galatians, Romans, recording any thoughts on the Daily Reading Journal pages.

WEEK 3

1–2 Corinthians, Galatians, Romans

1 CORINTHIANS

This letter is Paul's response to a letter he received from the church he founded in Corinth. He addresses several questions they asked him, and he also challenges some of their practices. While we no longer have the Corinthians' original letter to Paul, it appears from his responses that the following were some of the issues in the church:

- They were dividing into factions devoted to one or another of the early Christian leaders. These factions were modeled after the exclusive schools that gathered around philosophers of the day.
- They had misunderstood or misapplied Paul's earlier advice about how to deal with people in their community who were living immoral lives.
- They had adopted the Greek idea that the physical world is bad, so they wanted to free the human spirit from the body. One way they were trying to do this was by denying the body its pleasures.
- This desire had led some of the believers to deny the resurrection.
- Some of them wanted to keep attending ceremonial meals held in honor of pagan gods. They argued their participation in these meals was spiritually harmless because these weren't real gods.

- They were eager to receive the gift of speaking in tongues—to speak in another language without having to study it first—and use it in worship. But they were confused when some began saying things like "Jesus be cursed."
- They were taking one another to court in lawsuits.
- There was a dispute about wearing head-coverings in worship.
- When the community gathered for the Lord's Supper, a shared meal, the rich were eating by themselves, leaving the poor to go hungry.

What to watch for in 1 Corinthians: This letter is not for the faint of heart. At times, Paul is intense, angry, and even sarcastic. The church in Corinth was on the brink of destroying itself, and he loved them too much to let them stay on their downward slide.

2 CORINTHIANS

Paul experienced a great deal of conflict with the church he started in Corinth. They accused Paul of not being true to his word and appear to have challenged his leadership. Eventually, Paul learned from Titus they had reaffirmed their respect for his authority. In response, Paul wrote 2 Corinthians to reassure them as well as address some new problems:

- Paul reassured the Corinthians that all was now forgiven.
- He explain why he had changed his travel plans yet again.
- He encouraged them to continue to take up an offering they had begun to assist the poor—an effort that appears to have stalled.
- He responded to a threat of traveling Jewish-Christian teachers who had come to Corinth and were calling themselves super-apostles.

What to watch for in 2 Corinthians: Watch for the recurring theme of God's comfort in all our affliction. Paul uses the word *comfort* thirteen times in this letter.

GALATIANS

Paul wrote this letter to Gentile believers in Galatia (modern-day Turkey) to refute the idea they had to observe Jewish customs in order to be saved. This idea had evidently been spread by Jewish-Christian agitators who had visited the region and were claiming Paul had relaxed these restrictions just to get on their good side. In response to these charges:

- Paul insists the gospel he preached when he was with them was received directly by revelation from Jesus Christ. He is not trying to gain their favor.
- He reaffirms that faith in the Messiah alone is the basis of membership in God's new community. The Gentile believers thus do not need to be circumcised or try to keep other key provisions of the Jewish law.
- He explains that in place of the law, the Holy Spirit now lives inside the believers, giving them the power and the desire to live as God wishes.
- He describes the character qualities that make up the fruit of the Spirit and how these qualities should be lived out in the community of Jesus-followers.

What to watch for in Galatians: Notice how Paul connects Jesus to the story of Israel, arguing that all who follow Christ are children of Abraham.

ROMANS

Unlike Paul's earlier letters, he addresses Romans to a group of believers whom he had not met before. His purpose in writing is to introduce himself and gain the church's assistance in helping him spread the gospel to the western regions of the Roman Empire. To do this, Paul defends his credentials and explains the message of the gospel that he has been preaching:

- Paul proclaims boldly that he is an apostle, set apart to make the royal announcement about the Lordship of Jesus to the world.
- He explains that humanity is in slavery due to the entrance of sin and death to the world, but God has come to rescue both Jews and Gentiles.
- He states that God's plan for the world has been revealed in the life, death and resurrection of Jesus, the Messiah.
- He faces the difficult question of why many within Israel fail to believe in Jesus as the Messiah. Within the larger purposes of God, it turns out that Israel's rejection of Jesus has actually brought life to the rest of the world.
- He challenges the Romans to live the kind of new life, both individually and in community, that shows they've been restored to fellowship with God.

What to watch for in Romans: Romans is one of the most hotly debated books in the New Testament. Keep in mind that the purpose of all the complex theology is to call Gentiles to "the obedience that comes from faith."

PERSONAL BIBLE EXPERIENCE

Your personal Bible experience starts with a daily practice of reading the Bible. This week before your group meeting, read the books of 1–2 Corinthians, Galatians, and half of Romans. Use the journaling space to capture your thoughts, questions, responses, emotions, and insights as you read the daily selection. Keep in mind the following questions you will be talking about with your discussion group:

- What was new or compelling to you?
- What questions did you have?
- Was there anything that bothered you?
- What did you learn about loving God?
- What did you learn about loving others?

DAILY READING JOURNAL

Day 11: 1 Corinthians Invitation–7:40 (pages 121–131)

Day 12: 1 Corinthians 8:1–16:24 (pages 131–142)

Day 13: 2 Corinthians Invitation–13:14 (pages 143–157)

Day 14: Galatians Invitation–6:18 (pages 159–169)

Day 15: Romans Invitation–8:39 (pages 171–186)

COMMUNITY BIBLE EXPERIENCE

Welcome to week 3 of the Community Bible Experience. You have been experiencing the Bible personally by reading through the books of 1–2 Corinthians, Galatians, and half of Romans this week, and now your group has gathered to experience the Bible in community with each other. Think of your discussion as more of a book club than a Bible study.

REFLECTING ON THE PREVIOUS WEEK (30–60 minutes)

From your Personal Bible Experience in 1–2 Corinthians, Galatians, and Romans this week, have a conversation with your group about what you read by answering the following questions:

What was new or compelling to you?

What questions did you have?

Was there anything that bothered you?

What did you learn about loving God?

What did you learn about loving others?

PREPARING FOR THE WEEK AHEAD (15–20 minutes)

To get the most out of what you will be reading in the coming week, close your time together by watching the video for week 4, in which Jeff Manion explains the themes and relevance of **Romans, Colossians, Ephesians, Philemon, Philippians, 1 Timothy, Titus** and **2 Timothy**. Use the following outline to write down any insights or questions.

Prison Epistles

COLOSSIANS

Purpose of Colossians

To encourage growing faith, but growing faith is threatened faith

> So then, just as you received Christ Jesus as Lord, continue to live your lives in him, rooted and built up in him, strengthened in the faith as you were taught, and overflowing with thankfulness.
>
> (Colossians 2:6–7)

EPHESIANS

First half of Ephesians: Belonging and indicative

Second half of Ephesians: Commands and imperatives

Image of belonging: Adoption

Message of Ephesians: Belonging first, behavior second

Paul's plea to Philemon to restore the runaway slave, Onesimus

PHILIPPIANS

Thanks for the gift and friendship

Problem: Addressed selfishness

Relevance of Philippians

When we are where we don't want to be, God can use our lives powerfully.

Learn to say, "God, I will trust you in this place."

Pastoral Epistles

1 TIMOTHY

Topics in 1 Timothy

Qualifications for elders

Guidance for rich believers

> But godliness with contentment is great gain. For we brought nothing into the world, and we can take nothing out of it.
> (1 Timothy 6:6–7)

> Command those who are rich in this present world not to be arrogant nor to put their hope in wealth, which is so uncertain, but to put their hope in God, who richly provides us with everything for our enjoyment.
> (1 Timothy 6:17)

Relevance of 1 Timothy

Guidance for an affluent culture

TITUS

Message of Titus

Believers' behavior can influence unbelievers' perception of Jesus

> Teach slaves to be subject to their masters in everything, to try to please them, not to talk back to them, and not to steal from them, but to show that they can be fully trusted, so that in every way they will make the teaching about God our Savior attractive.
>
> (Titus 2:9–10)

Relevance of Titus

The way we live reflects on the reputation of Jesus

2 TIMOTHY

Relevance of 2 Timothy

God can transform hearts

THIS WEEK

Read the last part of Romans and the books of Colossians, Ephesians, Philemon, Philippians, 1 Timothy, Titus, and 2 Timothy in *The Books of the Bible: New Testament*. Maintain your momentum by keeping these guidelines in mind:

- Read what you can.
- Read something every day.
- Always have your *Books of the Bible* with you.
- Remember every week is a new week.
- Use this study journal as you do your reading for week 4: Romans, Colossians, Ephesians, Philemon, Philippians, 1 Timothy, Titus, 2 Timothy, recording any thoughts on the Daily Reading Journal pages.

WEEK 4

Romans, Colossians, Ephesians, Philemon, Philippians, 1 Timothy, Titus, 2 Timothy

COLOSSIANS

While Paul was sitting in a Roman prison awaiting trial, he penned this letter to the church in Colossae (modern-day Turkey) to warn about those who insisted on religious observances, secret spiritual knowledge, or harsh treatment of the body as necessary for salvation. Paul touches on the following points to clear up their wrong beliefs:

- He reminds them of the message they've believed and stresses that Christ made everything, rules over everything, and is reconciling everything to God.
- He explains his own struggles and exertions are for their sake and for the sake of others like them, to bring them to spiritual maturity.
- He challenges them to see they already have everything they need in Jesus—and they don't need to add anything to what Christ has already done for them.
- He encourages them to see themselves as people who've entered into a new kind of life, in which their personal character and community relationships will be transformed.

- He stresses the prayerful attitude the community should have as it seeks to bring the message about Jesus to others.

What to watch for in Colossians: Notice how Paul alternates between pragmatic exhortation and lyrical prose. It's thought the paragraph starting at the end of page 199, "The Son is the image of the invisible God . . ." is an early hymn to the supremacy of Christ.

EPHESIANS

Paul intended this to be a general letter circulated among the churches of Asia Minor (modern-day Turkey), to encourage Gentile converts to replace their old way of life with one of purity and integrity. Some of Paul's themes include the following:

- God raised Christ from the dead and seated him at his right hand in the heavenly realms, far above all rule and authority. In this way, God brought everything together under the rule of Jesus the Messiah.
- Jesus fulfills the original human calling to rule over the creation properly.
- Jews and Gentiles have been brought together into one body, with Jesus at the head. Gentiles who believe in Jesus are no longer foreigners and strangers but fellow citizens with God's people and members of his household.
- Believers in Christ must give up their former way of life and practice purity in daily living and integrity in their relationships.
- Believers have entered into a spiritual battle, so they must be on their guard and arm themselves with the resources God has provided—the armor of God.

What to watch for in Ephesians: Look for recurring themes from Paul's other letters, such as the relationship between Jewish and Gentile believers (see Romans), or the supremacy of Christ (see Colossians).

PHILEMON

Philemon was a wealthy man living in Colossae, whose slave, Onesimus, had run away. While on the run, Onesimus had put his faith in Jesus and become Paul's assistant. Paul sent him back to face his former master, this letter in hand, with these words to Philemon:

- He pleads with Philemon to welcome Onesimus back not as a slave but as a brother in Christ.
- He doesn't put Philemon under any obligation but appeals to him solely on the basis of love.
- He promises to honor the demands of justice by making whatever restitution Philemon required.

What to watch for in Philemon: Notice how Paul employs every ounce of persuasion to prevail upon Philemon.

PHILIPPIANS

The believers in Philippi (modern-day Greece) were some of Paul's most loyal supporters as well as his fellow-sufferers. His kinship with them was particularly poignant as he wrote to them from a Roman prison. In this letter, he offers them some challenges and encouragement:

- He knows the Philippians are experiencing opposition, just as he is, so he appeals to his own life as an example

of how they should respond. His desire is for them to be confident to proclaim the gospel without fear.
- He also knows some people in the community are having trouble getting along, so he urges them to have the same servant attitude as Jesus, who humbled himself to the point of death—all for the sake of others.
- He states they don't need to be circumcised, as some were teaching, and warns them not to live like those who are controlled by their desires.
- He urges them to rejoice in the partnership they have in helping others meet Jesus and in the reward they can anticipate when their work is finished.

What to watch for in Philippians: Notice how many times Paul mentions *joy* in Philippians, which is remarkable given that both the author and recipients of the letter were experiencing severe persecution.

1 TIMOTHY, TITUS, AND 2 TIMOTHY

Paul's final letters were written to his two young protégés to help them bring order to the renegade churches where they were ministering. Timothy was serving in Ephesus. The believers there were misapplying some Jewish practices and borrowing others from the philosophies of the day to create a regimen they expected believers to follow. In Paul's first letter to Timothy:

- He urges the community to respect those in authority and strive for peaceful and godly lives—the opposite of the chaos the upstart leaders were creating.
- He explains what kind of people the community should have as its leaders, so it can reject those who aren't qualified and replace them with those who are.

- He addresses a particular problem in the church of younger widows spreading bad influences. He states only godly older widows should be supported, while younger widows should remarry and devote themselves to family life.
- He ends with a special warning to the community to avoid greed.

Titus was serving on the island of Crete, and a similar situation was occurring there among the leadership as was happening in Ephesus. Thus, in Paul's letter to Titus:

- He describes the proper qualifications for community leadership.
- He identifies the teaching that must be opposed, showing how it was making the believers unfit for doing anything good.
- He instructs the community on how they can live out their varying stations in life and stresses how they can and should do what is good.

In Paul's second letter to Timothy, it is clear the situation in Ephesus had not improved, and it is likely Timothy was feeling discouraged. Thus, in Paul's second letter to Timothy:

- He encourages him to stay faithful to the true message—even if it meant suffering or death—and avoid false teaching.
- He reminds Timothy that in the last days, false teachers and persecutors will challenge the faithfulness of Jesus-followers.
- He urges Timothy to remember the gospel message: Jesus Christ, raised from the dead, descended from David.

- He points out the sacred writings Timothy has known since he was a child are God-breathed and will equip him for every good work.

What to watch for in 1 Timothy, Titus and 2 Timothy: Look for a different side to Paul's character than has been evident in other letters. Rather than the fierce leader, we see the affectionate mentor and fatherly friend.

PERSONAL BIBLE EXPERIENCE

Your personal Bible experience starts with a daily practice of reading the Bible. This week before your group meeting, read the last part of Romans and the books of Colossians, Ephesians, Philemon, Philippians, 1 Timothy, Titus, and 2 Timothy. Use the journaling space to capture your thoughts, questions, responses, emotions, and insights as you read the daily selection. Keep in mind the following questions you will be talking about with your discussion group:

- What was new or compelling to you?
- What questions did you have?
- Was there anything that bothered you?
- What did you learn about loving God?
- What did you learn about loving others?

DAILY READING JOURNAL

Day 16: Romans 9:1–16:27 (pages 186–196)

Day 17: Colossians Invitation–4:18 (pages 197–203)

Day 18: Ephesians Invitation–Philemon 25 (pages 205–218)

Day 19: Philippians Invitation–1 Timothy 6:21 (pages 219–234)

Day 20: Titus Invitation–2 Timothy 4:22 (pages 235–247)

COMMUNITY BIBLE EXPERIENCE

Welcome to week 4 of the Community Bible Experience. You have been experiencing the Bible personally by reading the last part of Romans and the books of Colossians, Ephesians, Philemon, Philippians, 1 Timothy, Titus, and 2 Timothy this week, and now your group has gathered to experience the Bible in community with each other. Think of your discussion as more of a book club than a Bible study.

REFLECTING ON THE PREVIOUS WEEK (30–60 minutes)

From your Personal Bible Experience in Romans, Colossians, Ephesians, Philemon, Philippians, 1 Timothy, Titus, and 2 Timothy this week, have a conversation with your group about what you read by answering the following questions:

What was new or compelling to you?

What questions did you have?

Was there anything that bothered you?

What did you learn about loving God?

What did you learn about loving others?

PREPARING FOR THE WEEK AHEAD (15–20 minutes)

To get the most out of what you will be reading in the coming week, close your time together by watching the video for week 5, in which Jeff Manion explains the themes and relevance of **Matthew**. Use the following outline to write down any insights or questions.

MATTHEW

Matthew—called from being a tax collector to a follower of Christ

Matthew's banquet for the tax collectors and sinners

> "For the Son of Man came to seek and to save the lost."
> (Luke 19:10)

Relevance of Matthew

It doesn't matter what you have done; Christ calls you to follow him.

Themes of Matthew

Fulfillment of prophecy

Jesus's life replicating the history of Israel—Jesus as founder of a restored Israel

Non-Jewish people coming to Jesus

Then Jesus came to them and said, "All authority in heaven and on earth has been given to me. Therefore go and make disciples of all nations, baptizing them in the name of the Father and of the Son and of the Holy Spirit, and teaching them to obey everything I have commanded you. And surely I am with you always, to the very end of the age."
(Matthew 28:18–20)

Jesus's authority

Relevance of Matthew

Does Christ have authority over you?

THIS WEEK

Read the book of Matthew in *The Books of the Bible: New Testament*. Maintain your momentum by keeping these guidelines in mind:

- Read what you can.
- Read something every day.
- Always have your *Books of the Bible* with you.
- Remember every week is a new week.
- Use this study journal as you do your reading for week 5: Matthew, recording any thoughts on the Daily Reading Journal pages.

WEEK 5
MATTHEW

MATTHEW

Matthew, the beginning of the second group of books in the New Testament, tells the story of Jesus from a Jewish perspective, presenting him as Israel's promised Messiah. The book does this by drawing a number of parallels between Jesus and Moses, including:

- They both narrowly escaped an attempt on their lives as infants.
- Moses spent forty years in the wilderness before his ministry. Jesus spent forty days in the wilderness before his ministry.
- Moses gave people the Torah, which was divided into five books. Matthew organizes the teachings of Jesus into five long speeches.
- Moses went up Mount Sinai to receive the law. Jesus gave his first speech on a mountain.
- Moses instituted the Passover. Jesus became the ultimate Passover lamb.

What to watch for in Matthew: Look for the five speeches of Jesus (which each end with, "When Jesus had finished saying these things . . ."), and notice how the events leading up to the speech tie in to each of the five themes.

PERSONAL BIBLE EXPERIENCE

Your personal Bible experience starts with a daily practice of reading the Bible. This week before your group meeting, read the book of Matthew. Use the journaling space to capture your thoughts, questions, responses, emotions, and insights as you read the daily selection. Keep in mind the questions you will be talking about with your discussion group:

- What was new or compelling to you?
- What questions did you have?
- Was there anything that bothered you?
- What did you learn about loving God?
- What did you learn about loving others?

DAILY READING JOURNAL

Day 21: Matthew Invitation–7:29 (pages 249–263)

Day 22: Matthew 8:1–13:52 (pages 263–275)

Day 23: Matthew 13:53–18:35 (pages 275–283)

Day 24: Matthew 19:1–25:46 (pages 283–296)

Day 25: Matthew 26:1–28:20 (pages 296–303)

COMMUNITY BIBLE EXPERIENCE

Welcome to week 5 of the Community Bible Experience. You have been experiencing the Bible personally by reading through the book of Matthew this week, and now your group has gathered to experience the Bible in community with each other. Think of your discussion as more of a book club than a Bible study.

REFLECTING ON THE PREVIOUS WEEK (30–60 minutes)

From your Personal Bible Experience in Matthew this week, have a conversation with your group about what you read by answering the following questions:

What was new or compelling to you?

What questions did you have?

Was there anything that bothered you?

What did you learn about loving God?

What did you learn about loving others?

PREPARING FOR THE WEEK AHEAD (15–20 minutes)

To get the most out of what you will be reading in the coming week, close your time together by watching the video for week 6, in which Jeff Manion explains the themes and relevance of **Hebrews**, **James**, and **Mark**. Use the following outline to write down any insights or questions.

HEBREWS

Written to Jewish believers suffering intense persecution

> Sometimes you were publicly exposed to insult and persecution; at other times you stood side by side with those who were so treated. You suffered along with those in prison and joyfully accepted the confiscation of your property.
> (Hebrews 10:33–34)

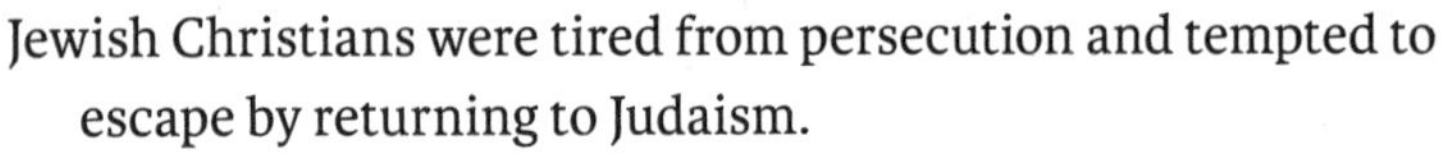

Jewish Christians were tired from persecution and tempted to escape by returning to Judaism.

Purpose of Hebrews

Draws the contrast between the old system and Jesus's new system

To encourage perseverance

Recall heroes of the faith (Hebrews 11)

Relevance of Hebrews

The journey of following God has always been a journey of trust.

JAMES

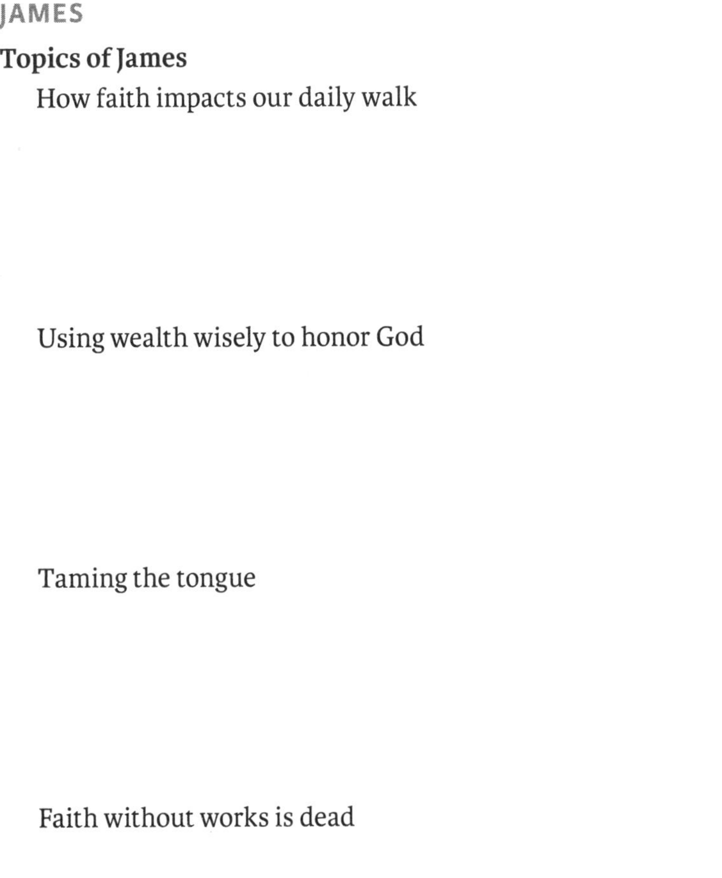

Topics of James

How faith impacts our daily walk

Using wealth wisely to honor God

Taming the tongue

Faith without works is dead

Relevance of James

Scripture is intended not for information but transformation.

Ask: How am I allowing the Word of God to transform my life?

MARK

The writer of action

Writing to a Gentile audience in Rome, Mark is intent on communicating Jesus clearly in different cultural contexts.

Focus of Mark

Mark presents Jesus's authority.

One-third of Mark is spent on Jesus's death.

Jesus's suffering for us can encourage perseverance in persecution.

Relevance of Hebrews, James, and Mark

Persevere and cling to Christ.

THIS WEEK

Read the books of Hebrews, James, and Mark in *The Books of the Bible: New Testament*. Maintain your momentum by keeping these guidelines in mind:

- Read what you can.
- Read something every day.
- Always have your *Books of the Bible* with you.
- Remember every week is a new week.
- Use this study journal as you do your reading for week 6: Hebrews, James, Mark, recording any thoughts on the Daily Reading Journal pages.

WEEK 6

HEBREWS, JAMES, MARK

HEBREWS

The author of Hebrews doesn't give his name or state to whom he is writing. However, the recipients are clearly Jews who have come to believe in Jesus as their Messiah. These believers are being tempted to escape persecution by identifying themselves as Jews rather than as followers of Jesus. The author warns them not to do this, stressing four key points:

- Jesus is much greater than the angels, so the salvation he announced is much greater than the message spoken through angels, that is, in the law of Moses.
- Jesus is our apostle. Moses and Joshua brought the Israelites into the Promised Land, but the promised land Jesus brings us into is a much greater.
- Jesus is our high priest, and his advocacy for us in that position is much more effective than that of the priests appointed by the law of Moses.
- We must respond to all that God has done through Jesus by stepping out in faith—that is, by living in light of unseen heavenly realities.

What to watch for in Hebrews: With its rich imagery and complex theology, Hebrews is one of the most challenging books to read in the New Testament. If you find yourself getting bogged down, focus on the call in the last section (pages 319–324) to respond to all God has done for us by stepping out in faith.

JAMES

James, one of the brothers of Jesus, addressed this letter to Jewish believers scattered throughout the Roman Empire. The book is made up of a collection of short sayings, perhaps ones that James repeated as he advised people. Some of the topics include:

- Wisdom is demonstrated in practical conduct. The wisdom that comes from heaven is first of all pure; then peace-loving, considerate, submissive, full of mercy and good fruit, impartial, and sincere.
- Believers must be concerned for the poor and use wealth responsibly.
- Believers must control their tongue and speech, maintain purity in life, and have unity within the community of Jesus-followers.
- Above all, believers must have patience and endurance during times of trial.

What to watch for in James: This book should be read not like the epistles, which were letters, but like the book of Proverbs and Ecclesiastes, which were a collection of sayings. Be sure to slow down and allow time to ponder each nugget of wisdom.

MARK

The book of Mark begins the third group of New Testament books: those written or influenced by Peter. Mark was written to a Roman audience and appears to be the memoirs of Peter, who was Mark's fellow ministry partner. Mark highlights the importance of being willing to suffer for Jesus. In his book, the tension centers around the identity of Jesus and builds in several acts:

- In the first act, Jesus teaches and heals the crowds that swarm to him.
- In the second act, Jesus encounters more conflict and opposition.
- In the third act, the disciples struggle more to understand who Jesus is.
- In the fourth act, Jesus travels to Jerusalem, where he teaches in the temple and clashes with the established leadership. This leadership executes its plan and has Jesus arrested and crucified, seemingly "overturning" all he has done.
- In the final act, God "overturns" their deed and raises Jesus to life.

What to watch for in Mark: Mark is a master storyteller, and his Gospel moves at a breakneck speed. Try reading this book as quickly as you comfortably can, and allow yourself to get caught up in the building tension of this action-packed drama.

PERSONAL BIBLE EXPERIENCE

Your personal Bible experience starts with a daily practice of reading the Bible. This week before your group meeting, read the books of Hebrews, James, and Mark. Use the journaling space to capture your thoughts, questions, responses, emotions, and insights as you read the daily selection. Keep in mind the questions you will be talking about with your discussion group:

- What was new or compelling to you?
- What questions did you have?
- Was there anything that bothered you?
- What did you learn about loving God?
- What did you learn about loving others?

DAILY READING JOURNAL

Day 26: Hebrews Invitation–4:13 (pages 305–311)

Day 27: Hebrews 4:14–13:25 (pages 311–324)

Day 28: James Invitation–5:20 (pages 325–332)

Day 29: Mark Invitation–8:30 (pages 333–351)

Day 30: Mark 8:31–16:20 (pages 351–367)

COMMUNITY BIBLE EXPERIENCE

Welcome to week 6 of the Community Bible Experience. You have been experiencing the Bible personally by reading through the books of Hebrews, James, and Mark this week, and now your group has gathered to experience the Bible in community with each other. Think of your discussion as more of a book club than a Bible study.

REFLECTING ON THE PREVIOUS WEEK (30–60 minutes)

From your Personal Bible Experience in Hebrews, James, and Mark this week, have a conversation with your group about what you read by answering the following questions:

What was new or compelling to you?

What questions did you have?

Was there anything that bothered you?

What did you learn about loving God?

What did you learn about loving others?

PREPARING FOR THE WEEK AHEAD (15–20 minutes)

To get the most out of what you will be reading in the coming week, close your time together by watching the video for week 7, in which Jeff Manion explains the themes and relevance of **1–2 Peter**, **Jude**, and **John**. Use the following outline to write down any insights or questions.

1 PETER

Peter's darkest moment: His betrayal. Then Jesus restores Peter.

Relevance: Jesus is not done with us yet, no matter the failure

Peter writes thirty years after the crucifixion

Focus of 1 Peter

Our high calling as children of God and a call to live a holy life

Persecution and how to endure it, based on the example of Jesus's manner of suffering

2 PETER AND JUDE

New crisis: Is Jesus coming back?

Jesus will keep his promise to return and will restore the world.

Relevance of 1–2 Peter and Jude

Live lives that are separated to God.

JOHN

Structure of John

Synoptic Gospels: Matthew, Mark, and Luke

John includes different material and perspective.

Cadence of John: Miracle followed by speech or sermon

John opens with the same words as Genesis: "In the beginning . . ."

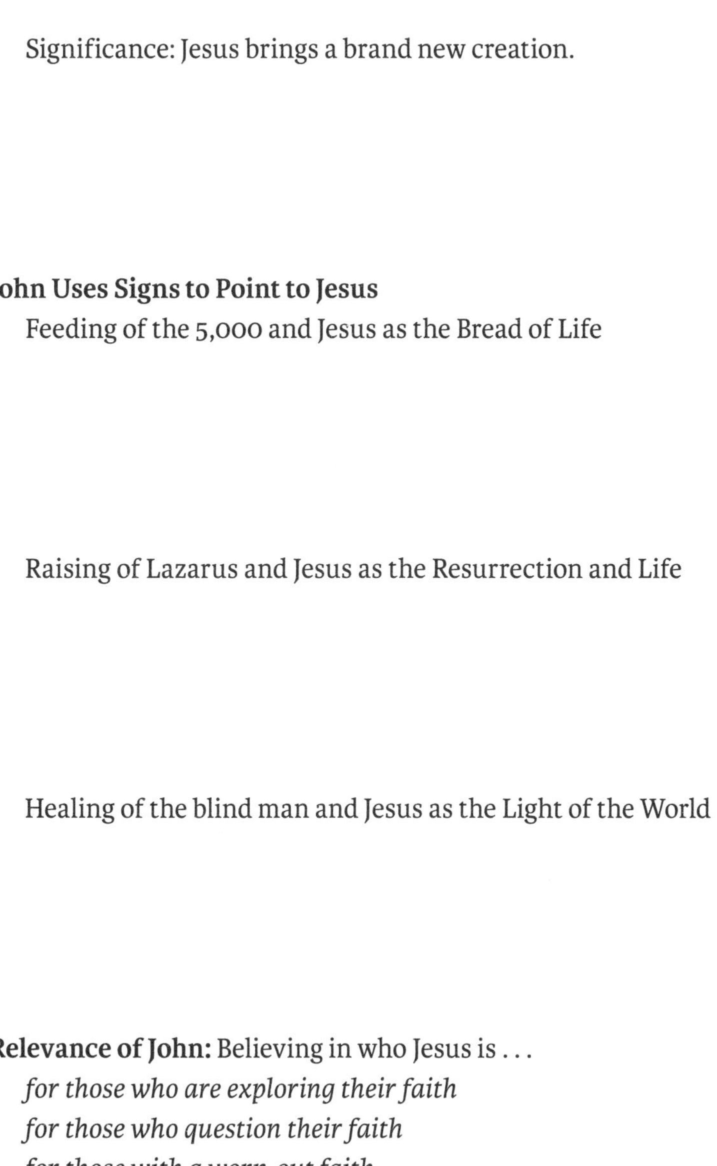

Significance: Jesus brings a brand new creation.

John Uses Signs to Point to Jesus

Feeding of the 5,000 and Jesus as the Bread of Life

Raising of Lazarus and Jesus as the Resurrection and Life

Healing of the blind man and Jesus as the Light of the World

Relevance of John: Believing in who Jesus is . . .

for those who are exploring their faith

for those who question their faith

for those with a worn-out faith

THIS WEEK

Read the books of 1–2 Peter, Jude, and John in *The Books of the Bible: New Testament*. Maintain your momentum by keeping these guidelines in mind:

- Read what you can.
- Read something every day.
- Always have your *Books of the Bible* with you.
- Remember every week is a new week.
- Use this study journal as you do your reading for week 7: 1–2 Peter, Jude, and John, recording any thoughts on the Daily Reading Journal pages.

WEEK 7
1–2 Peter, Jude, John

1 PETER

Peter wrote letters to encourage Gentile believers in what is now Turkey. The main point of his first letter is to encourage believers to remain faithful in the face of intense persecution. His first letter consists of the following three main sections:

- Peter tells them to be holy in all they do. He reminds them that as Gentiles, they once lived in ignorance (they didn't know the ways of God). But they are now a holy nation, part of God's own people, and called to a new way of life.
- Peter describes one effect of this way of life: it will impress those who would persecute them. This must be achieved practically, in human relationships.
- Peter explains their suffering is to be expected. Jesus himself suffered, and their fellow believers throughout the world are undergoing the same kind of sufferings, so they should bear up patiently and faithfully.

What to watch for in 1 Peter: Think of Peter's own story as you read about suffering for the faith. This is the man who caved under the scrutiny of a servant girl! How far he has come. He now deeply understands both the irony of his own history and the dichotomy of being able to rejoice as one participates in the sufferings of Christ.

2 PETER AND JUDE

Peter's second letter addresses false teachings who were contending that because Jesus had not returned already, his return couldn't be expected at all—and thus believers were free to lead immoral lives. (Peter likely heard about this threat from the letter sent by Jude, as both address the same issue). Peter stresses the following key points in this letter:

- He stresses that he, along with James and John, personally saw the glory and majesty of Jesus when they were with him on the sacred mountain. All believers will see this same glory when Jesus returns.
- Peter reminds his readers that the prophetic message in the Scriptures testifies to Jesus's return as well.
- He observes that false teachers have slipped in among the people of God throughout their history, so his readers shouldn't be surprised this is also happening in their own day. A judgment awaits these false teachers.
- He explains the Messiah is indeed coming back, but his return has been delayed, because God is not wanting anyone to perish.

Jude was another brother of Jesus. As previously noted, his letter addresses the same concerns that Peter raised in his second letter:

- Jude warns about false teachers who were threatening the faith once for all entrusted to God's holy people.
- Even though these teachers claim to bring God's message, they are merely following natural instincts and do not have the Spirit.

- The believers' response to them must be active resistance. They must contend for the faith by rejecting both the teaching and the example of these men.

What to watch for in 2 Peter and Jude: As you read, think about how you can "contend for the faith" while giving people space to process their doubts and ask honest questions.

JOHN

The book of John marks the fourth and final group of New Testament books. According to John, he wrote his Gospel "that you may believe that Jesus is the Messiah, the Son of God, and that by believing you may have life in his name" (John 20:31). The issue of belief is thus central to John's purpose in telling Jesus's story. John reveals Jesus's divine identity by recording seven instances in which Jesus referred to himself as "I am," which in the Old Testament was the name for God:

- "I am" the bread of life.
- "I am" the light of the world.
- "I am" the gate for the sheep.
- "I am" the good shepherd.
- "I am" the resurrection and the life.
- "I am" the way, the truth, and the life.
- "I am" the true vine.

What to watch for in John: Notice how the number *seven* appears in other ways in John's gospel. For instance, you will read of seven miracles that Jesus performs. To the Jewish people, the number *seven* represented completeness or wholeness—a finished work of God.

PERSONAL BIBLE EXPERIENCE

Your personal Bible experience starts with a daily practice of reading the Bible. This week before your group meeting, read the books of 1–2 Peter, Jude, and John. Use the journaling space to capture your thoughts, questions, responses, emotions, and insights as you read the daily selection. Keep in mind the questions you will be talking about with your discussion group:

- What was new or compelling to you?
- What questions did you have?
- Was there anything that bothered you?
- What did you learn about loving God?
- What did you learn about loving others?

DAILY READING JOURNAL

Day 31: 1 Peter Invitation–5:14 (pages 369–376)

Day 32: 2 Peter Invitation–Jude 25 (pages 377–386)

Day 33: John Invitation–6:71 (pages 387–403)

Day 34: John 7:1–12:50 (pages 403–416)

Day 35: John 13:1–21:25 (pages 416–430)

COMMUNITY BIBLE EXPERIENCE

Welcome to session 7 of the Community Bible Experience. You have been experiencing the Bible personally by reading through the books of 1–2 Peter, Jude, and John this week, and now your group has gathered to experience the Bible in community with each other. Think of your discussion as more of a book club than a Bible study.

REFLECTING ON THE PREVIOUS WEEK (30–60 minutes)

From your Personal Bible Experience in 1–2 Peter, Jude, and John this week, have a conversation with your group about what you read by answering the following questions:

What was new or compelling to you?

What questions did you have?

Was there anything that bothered you?

What did you learn about loving God?

What did you learn about loving others?

PREPARING FOR THE WEEK AHEAD (15–20 minutes)

To get the most out of what you will be reading in the coming week, close your time together by watching the video for week 8, in which Jeff Manion explains the themes and relevance of **1–3 John** and **Revelation**. Use the following outline to write down any insights or questions.

1 JOHN

Problems addressed in 1 John:

Gnosticism and denial of Jesus's physical body—but we saw Jesus with our own eyes

Belief that sin is of no consequence—but you are called to holiness in your body

Disregard of loving others—let us love one another

2–3 JOHN

How to deal with those causing these problems:

2 John: Warning against false teachers

3 John: Open your homes to the true teachers

Relevance of 1–3 John

Jesus knows what it means to be human.

The importance of love

REVELATION

Revelation uses apocalyptic literature, which paints a picture of the seen and unseen world, and the unveiling of the conflict.

Opening Messages from Jesus to Congregations

Affirmation and correction

Jesus's concern for the life and health of the church

Characters in Revelation

The main character is God himself.

Jesus is shown as both the Suffering Servant and Coming King.

Relevance of Revelation

Absorb how the story ends in re-creation.

Bible begins with the presence of God and the loss of his presence, and ends with God's presence returning.

THIS WEEK

Read the books of 1–3 John and Revelation in *The Books of the Bible: New Testament*. Maintain your momentum by keeping these guidelines in mind:

- Read what you can.
- Read something every day.
- Always have your *Books of the Bible* with you.
- Remember every week is a new week.
- Use this study journal as you do your reading for week 8: 1–3 John, Revelation, recording any thoughts on the Daily Reading Journal pages.

WEEK 8

1–3 John, Revelation

1, 2, 3 JOHN

John's letters give us a good picture of the church toward the end of the first century, which in some cases was a church embroiled in controversy. In John's first letter, he addresses a Greek philosophy that contended all flesh is evil and only spirit is good. John counters this teaching stating that if this were so, then how could God have come to earth in a human body? And why would we need to live moral lives? John weaves together several main themes:

- He testifies to the reality of the Son of God's coming in the flesh.
- He warns believers not to let anyone deceive them and refutes the claims of those who have left the main teachings of the gospel.
- He reassures believers they have full access to the truth.
- He emphasizes godly living and practical caring as the signs of those who genuinely know God.

John's second letter is to a different audience, but in it he also warns believers against listening to false teachers and tells them not to provide assistance to them. In his third letter, John takes the opposite approach, encouraging church members to extend hospitality toward those who are actually promoting the true message of Jesus.

What to watch for in 1–3 John: See if you notice any parallels or similar phrasing between John's letters and John's Gospel.

For example, *"This is how God showed his love among us: He sent his one and only Son into the world that we might live through him"* (1 John 4:9).

REVELATION

John received a vision toward the end of his life in which he saw that the cult of emperor worship would soon become deadly to followers of Jesus. He wrote down this vision in a literary form known as *apocalypse*, in which a visitor from heaven takes the recipient of the vision on a journey through heaven, using vivid symbols to disclose the secrets of the unseen world and the future. The vision enables the recipients to understand the spiritual dimensions of their situation and to respond to the crisis by remaining loyal to God. This vision that John records from heaven consists of four main parts:

- In the first part, John is in the Spirit on Patmos and receives a vision on the Lord's Day. In this vision, Jesus speaks words of warning and encouragement to each of the seven churches.
- In the second part, John sees Jesus being exalted because he had redeemed humanity through his sacrifice. He also sees Jesus begin to execute God's judgment against his enemies, while protecting those who belong to him.
- In the third part, John is taken in the Spirit to a wilderness, where he is shown the true spiritual state of the Roman Empire. Despite Rome's pretensions to glory, it is really drunken, greedy, blasphemous, immoral—and doomed. In this long vision, John also sees the triumph of the Messiah over his enemies.
- In the fourth part, John is taken in the Spirit onto a mountain, where he sees the new Jerusalem coming

down out of heaven. The vision closes with the promise that God's faithful servants will reign over the new creation.

What to watch for in Revelation: Revelation has some of the most puzzling imagery in the Bible. Whatever you make of its content, remember the key message: *Stand firm, because in the end, God wins.*

PERSONAL BIBLE EXPERIENCE

Your personal Bible experience starts with a daily practice of reading the Bible. This week before your group meeting, read the books of 1–3 John and Revelation. Use the journaling space to capture your thoughts, questions, responses, emotions, and insights as you read the daily selection. Keep in mind the questions you will be talking about with your discussion group:

- What was new or compelling to you?
- What questions did you have?
- Was there anything that bothered you?
- What did you learn about loving God?
- What did you learn about loving others?

DAILY READING JOURNAL

Day 36: 1 John Invitation–3 John 14 (pages 431–445)

Day 37: Revelation Invitation–3:22 (pages 447–455)

Day 38: Revelation 4:1–16:21 (pages 455–469)

Day 39: Revelation 17:1–22:21 (pages 469–477)

Day 40: Write down your main takeaways from this study and what you have learned now that you have finished reading through the entire New Testament

COMMUNITY BIBLE EXPERIENCE

Welcome to week 8 of the Community Bible Experience. You have been experiencing the Bible personally by reading through the books of 1–3 John and Revelation this week, and now your group has gathered to experience the Bible in community with each other. Think of your discussion as more of a book club than a Bible study.

REFLECTING ON THE PREVIOUS WEEK (30–60 minutes)

From your Personal Bible Experience in 1–3 John and Revelation this week, have a conversation with your group about what you read by answering the following questions:

What was new or compelling to you?

What questions did you have?

Was there anything that bothered you?

What did you learn about loving God?

What did you learn about loving others?

FINAL REFLECTIONS (15–30 minutes)

Reflect: Give each person a chance to share how their journey through the New Testament impacted them, how it shaped their understanding of the Bible, and what implications it might have for their life.

Rejoice: Celebrate your achievement together! Reading through *The Books of the Bible: New Testament* in just eight weeks is a major accomplishment. If you have read all four volumes in *The Books of the Bible* series, rejoice all the more! You have achieved a milestone some of you may have never thought possible. Take some time to thank each other for providing the community support and encouragement it took to finish this journey together.

Regroup: Plan your next meeting. If you want to continue studying the Bible in this series, consider going through *The Books of the Bible: Covenant History,* followed by *The Books of the Bible: The Prophets* and *The Books of the Bible: The Writing.* Going through each of these studies will give you a comprehensive look at the rest of the Bible . . . the Old Testament.

Leader's Guide

Thank you for your willingness to lead your group through this study! What you have chosen to do is important, and much good fruit can come from studies like this. The rewards of being a leader are different from those of participating, and we hope that as you lead your group, you will find your own walk with Jesus deepened by this experience.

The New Testament Challenge is an eight-week study built around video content and small-group interaction. As the group leader, imagine yourself as the host of a dinner party. Your job is to take care of your guests by managing all the behind-the-scenes details so that when everyone arrives, they can just enjoy time together.

As the group leader, your role is not to answer all the questions or reteach the content—the video, book, and study guide will do most of that work. Your job is to guide the experience and cultivate your small group into a kind of teaching community. This will make it a place for members to process, question, and reflect—not receive more instruction.

There are several elements in this leader's guide that will help you as you structure your study and reflection time, so follow along and take advantage of each one.

BEFORE YOU BEGIN

Before your first meeting, make sure the group members have a copy of this study guide so they can follow along and start reading if they desire to do so. Alternately, you can hand out the study guides at your first meeting and give the group members some time to look over the material and ask any preliminary questions. During your first meeting, be sure to send a sheet around the room and have the members write down their names, phone numbers, and email addresses so you can keep in touch with them during the week.

Generally, the ideal size for a group is between eight to ten people, which ensures everyone will have enough time to participate in discussions. If you have more people, you might want to break into smaller subgroups. Encourage those who show up at the first meeting to commit to attending the duration of the study, as this will help the group members get to know each other, create stability for the group, and help you know how to prepare each week.

Each of the sessions begins with the group members reflecting on the previous week's reading. During this time, your group will discuss the following five questions: (1) What was new or compelling to you? (2) What questions did you have? (3) Was there anything that bothered you? (4) What did you learn about loving God? (5) What did you learn about loving others? Let the group members know sharing is optional, and it's okay if they didn't get to all of the reading during the week. It will still be beneficial for them to hear from the other participants and learn about what they discovered.

WEEKLY PREPARATION

As the leader, there are a few things you should do to prepare for each meeting:

- *Read through the session.* This will help you to become familiar with the content and know how to structure the discussion times.
- *Be familiar with the questions.* When the group meets, you will be watching the clock, so you want to make

sure you are familiar with the questions. In this way, you will ensure that you have the material more deeply in your mind than your group members.

- *Pray for your group.* Pray for your group members throughout the week and ask God to lead them as they study his Word.
- *Bring extra supplies to your meeting.* The members should bring their own pens for writing notes, but it's a good idea to have extras available for those who forget. You may also want to bring paper and additional Bibles.

Note there will be no one "right" answer to the questions. Answers will vary, especially when the group members are being asked to share their personal experiences.

STRUCTURING THE DISCUSSION TIME

You will need to determine with your group how long you want to meet each week so you can plan your time accordingly. Generally, most groups like to meet for either sixty minutes or ninety minutes. Keep in mind each of the videos the group will be watching average around fifteen minutes in length, so the bulk of your time (approximately thirty to sixty minutes) will be spent discussing the five questions in the "Reflecting on the Previous Week" section, which cover the material the participants read during the week. (The rest of the time will generally be taken up with getting the group members settled in at the beginning of the session and wrapping up your time together at the end with prayer or other discussion.)

Remember that as the group leader, it is up to you to keep track of the time and keep things moving along according to your schedule. You might want to set a timer for each segment so both you and the group members know when your time is up. (Note there are some good phone apps for timers that play a gentle chime or other pleasant sound instead of a disruptive noise.) Finally, don't be concerned if the group members are quiet or slow to share. People are often quiet when they are pulling together their ideas, and this might be a new experience for them. Just ask a question and let it hang in the air until someone shares. You can then say, "Thank you. What about others?"

GROUP DYNAMICS

Leading a group through *The New Testament Challenge* will prove to be highly rewarding both to you and your group members. However, this doesn't mean you will not encounter any challenges along the way. Discussions can get off track. Group members may not be sensitive to the needs and ideas of others. Some might worry they will be expected to talk about matters that make them feel awkward. Others may express comments that result in disagreements. To help ease this strain on you and the group, consider the following ground rules:

- When someone raises a question or comment that is off topic, suggest you deal with it another time, or, if you feel led to go in that direction, let the group know you will be spending some time discussing it.
- If someone asks a question you don't know how to answer, admit it and move on. At your discretion, feel free to invite group members to comment on questions that call for personal experience.
- If you find one or two people are dominating the discussion time, direct a few questions to others in the group. Outside the main group time, ask the more dominating members to help you draw out the quieter ones. Work to make them a part of the solution instead of the problem.

- When a disagreement occurs, encourage the group members to process the matter in love. Encourage those on opposite sides to restate what they heard the other side say about the matter, and then invite each side to evaluate if that perception is accurate. Lead the group in examining other Scriptures related to the topic and look for common ground.

When any of these issues arise, encourage your group to follow these words from the Bible: "Love one another" (John 13:34), "If it is possible, as far as it depends on you, live at peace with everyone" (Romans 12:18), "Whatever is true . . . noble . . . pure . . . lovely . . . if anything is excellent or praiseworthy—think about such things" (Philippians 4:8), and "Be quick to listen, slow to speak, and slow to become angry" (James 1:19). This will make your group time more rewarding and beneficial for everyone who attends.

Thank you again for your willingness to lead your group. May God reward your efforts and dedication, equip you to guide your group in the weeks ahead, and make your time together in *The New Testament Challenge* fruitful for His kingdom.

— ALSO AVAILABLE —

Do you know the real story behind the New Testament?

Study Guide
9780310085263

DVD with
Free Streaming Access
9780310085287

Bible scholars N.T. Wright and Michael F. Bird team up to take you on a tour of the story behind the explosive story of the New Testament. You will discover things you never knew about Jesus' baptism and journey into the wilderness, the meaning behind his parables and miracles, the significance of his death and resurrection, the incredible expansion of the early church into the Greco-Roman world, and how the transforming mission of Jesus can still turn the world upside down today.

Available now at your favorite bookstore,
or streaming video on StudyGateway.com.

ZONDERVAN®